Broken Yet Healed

Azalea Marie

Arizona Book Publishing
www.ArizonaBookPublishing.com

Broken Yet Healed

Azalea Marie

Copyright © December 2024

Cover by Jacob Amaro

ISBN: 979-8-89443-865-8

INTRODUCTION

The abuse of young children is a silent epidemic that devastates countless lives each day. It affects 1 in 4 girls and 1 in 13 boys, a staggering reality that underscores the need to break the silence surrounding this issue.

In the U.S. alone, over one billion kids experience the horrors of sexual violence, leaving lasting scars.

As I share my story of pain, resilience, and healing, I want to express my deep gratitude to my husband for his unwavering support, my friends for their compassion, and my children for their laughter and love that remind me of life's beauty. To my family, thank you for your warmth and understanding in helping me rebuild.

To every child who has suffered abuse: know that what happened to you is not your fault, and the pain you carry does not define you. Together, we can shed light on these dark realities and foster a community of healing and hope. As you turn these pages, I hope you can use my life to find strength in your struggles and a renewed belief in the power of your own voice.

Contents

Part One: How Did I Ever Survive? 1

Part Two: What Finally Broke Me 21

Part Three: The Tipping Point 27

Part Four: Healing Begins 45

Part One: How Did I Ever Survive?

Imagine walking into a crime scene, but instead of a body, you find a tornado of chaos, with clothes strewn everywhere: on the floor, the dressers, the bed, and even the bathtub. Clean or dirty? Who could tell? They were everywhere! The kitchen was a battlefield with food on the counters, in the sink, and even in the rooms, making it smell like a delightful mix of feces, mildew, and spoiled milk with just a hint of broken dreams.

Every time someone came over, they thought we'd been robbed and ransacked by burglars, but no, that was just how we lived. I was so young and gullible that I believed every word my parents told me. To them, this was how a home was supposed to look!

Whenever my biological parents talked, they were always right when it came to our lifestyle.

Home after home, school after school, strangers in and out of the house every day that was the life of a poor girl and her family.

Through hardships, broken homes, torn families, and without a happy childhood, she always found a way to conjure a smile. She would always find a way to smile through everything, no matter how terrible it was, and truthfully, most of the time, she was in a dark, deep hole.

She felt like an ugly, broken, and unloved flower.

This girl was and is the strongest person I know.

I know this because that little girl was me.

I was born in Tucson, Arizona, to my birth parents on July 2, 1993, as the second oldest of five siblings: Shawn, Steven, Dyson, Casper, and Wally. We lived in Tucson until I was nine and then moved to New Mexico.

After that, we lived there until I was twelve, and then I returned to Tucson. I have lived here ever since.

Ever since I was little, I thought what was happening in my life was perfectly normal, but it was such a broken home that no matter what happened, nothing could ever fix it. Well, that is what I thought.

I did not think anything would ever be better, and because of that, I will always continue to have memories of my worst nightmares.

My biological parents are not the kind of parents I would recommend to anyone. They married when my mom was still pregnant with me. With each of us kids being born, my biological mom used to do a lot of drugs even when she was pregnant.

I am surprised we made it out alive.

My real mom lived a decent life until she met my real dad. She only smoked cigarettes and weed, but then she did a wild thing by losing her virginity at the age of thirteen and began sleeping with every guy she met.

She started skipping school and then began doing hardcore drugs. My birth father always had to have his fix of drugs, and my real mom needed her fix of sex.

They tried everything, including heroin.

The more they did drugs, the more they had sex with multiple people, which changed who they were.

Not realizing what they were doing when I was a little girl, other than making them happy, made me think it was okay, but my older brother did not feel like it was because of the drugs. According to our mommy and daddy, it was for the best, but starting when we could comprehend things and understand, which was in elementary school, he and I began to realize that life was not the same for us as it was for other kids.

It seemed as though we moved every two years to anywhere my parents felt was convenient, from shacks and trailers to hotels. My brothers and I are about two years apart. My older brother Shawn is now twenty-two, I'm twenty, Steven is sixteen, Dyson is fourteen, Casper is twelve, and Wally is about to be ten.

If all the kids that my real mother was pregnant with had lived, there would've been sixteen of us.

All the other siblings we might have had were either a miscarriage or born dead from being beaten or what my real mother did to her body with the drugs. I often wonder what it would be like to have so many siblings.

With each move we made, I thought it would bring our family closer, but each time we moved, our lives only got worse because wherever we lived, I always had to share a room with one of the boys.

Sometimes, if the place were small, we would all be in just two bedrooms on three different beds.

The living arrangements were inadequate because things just never got cleaned, having such a big family living in such a small area. The environment was also bad because the places my biological parents chose to live had drug dealers written all over them.

There were days we would have to sleep in the same clothes or wear the same outfits three times a week.

My real mom did not do much of anything, not because she did not know how, but clearly because she was lazy. My real dad did all the cooking, and even then, we would go without eating most of the time. If the food in the house was getting low, my older brother and I would give our food to the younger ones.

I do not remember when any of us had nice, clean clothes unless my aunt, uncle, grandpa, and grandma bought them. The only time the place ever got clean was because my older brother and I did the work.

Also, we lived with many animals, including dogs, cats, and even rats. Talk about a mini farm! I say that because we were always in the double digits with them.

One of my fondest memories of all our animals was of the little ones called roaches. We had so many nests because of all the animal feces and not having a clean place. Everything was so gross that when it came to our hair, we often got lice, and again, my parents did not clean us; my aunt and uncle did.

Living with all the dirty filth of clothes and our little animal friends in the place we called home was okay because it was a daily occurrence. We lived this way so long, not because we wanted to but because we had to.

I remember wanting friends to come over, but I was too embarrassed by roaches coming out everywhere. My brother and I would go to school unclean, with un-brushed teeth, and have foul smells on us from old sweat mixed with urine, feces, and a hint of gasoline.

It didn't bother my brother and me because we were so used to the smell, but to others, it was the worst.

My hair would always be greasy and have a mixture of stenches that hair should not smell like. Sometimes, I would have to wear my eldest brother's clothes.

If it wasn't for my older brothers' clothes, the way I'd dress was not an outfit a young girl should wear.

Picture a prostitute and now put that image on me. From about the ages of seven to twelve, my birth mother dressed me to look like a baby prostitute with half shirts and skirts and sometimes wore makeup with heels.

I did not know it was so bad because Mom said it was okay, but now, as I look back, I realize and think, "Oh my God, I can't believe my mother would dress me like that." I mean, she was supposed to be my role model, my mom, not some dealer pimping me out.

I would always go with my mom to get her sexual fix, and when she dressed as she did, sexual happenings occurred that nobody should have to face or even see at any age. She would promise me if I went with her, we would have better food, so hearing that was like heaven, but heaven turned into hell very quickly, and when I never got any food, at the end of the day, I would be more broken than when I started that same morning.

Speaking of food, it was tight, not because we did not have the money but because the money went on other things that were not as important. My biological mom made a lot of money from Social Security Income (SSI) because she told the government that each of her kids had been born with some disability. We could've lived a better and more decent life if my parents had used their heads better. Instead, the money was used for all sorts of drugs and for my mom to have sex.

When we did eat, it still wasn't very nutritional.

The majority of the food was junk and alcohol.

I have a few good memories of my birth father; for example, sometimes, we would go to the Burger King on Ajo and Palo Verde to get chocolate shakes with two cherries, and if the machine was down, he would drive to another one. That was always such a treat. I looked forward to it every Friday when he got paid.

Another delightful memory was a little antique shop near where we lived. I have always loved Christmas, with all the lights and decorations.

One year, I saved some money that was given to me and spent it on a one-foot-tall Christmas tree and some lights because that was all I wanted, but we had no ornaments, so our real dad took us to the antique shop, and we got to pick out a set of cute little ornaments.

I wanted a Tinkerbell ornament, which I loved, and so did my brother, but all the single ones cost more than the box. The lady who owned the shop was super sweet and would always say hello as we walked to school.

A few months later, she passed away, but she had arranged for a delivery to be sent to my siblings and me, which were the ornaments we each wanted. We were beyond happy until they got sold for drugs.

I remember the time we went grocery shopping. When we got to the register, my biological mom put everything back that we wanted and, instead, just got what she wanted, which was a bunch of junk.

We'd picked out juices and microwave dinners, but she bought donuts, brownies, soda, and candy.

"Mom, why can't we have what we picked out?" Shawn asked her.

"Mommy, you said it would be our turn to get what we wanted to eat." I reminded her.

"Mamma, I want juice, please," Steven begged.

"I am the parent and have the money, so I get to pick what we take home," she explained.

"But Mommy, we are hungry, and the things you picked aren't good for us," we all said.

"Just keep it up, and none of you will get fed at all," she yelled.

"Okay, Mom, sorry, we are just so hungry," Shawn whined, crying and wiping tears from his eyes.

"Please do not be mad at us, mama. You promised us last time we could pick whatever we wanted this time, and you broke it again," I said, also sobbing.

"You will eat what I give you and like it. That's it." Mother demanded, just as she always did.

Not only did we have SSI but also food stamps and WIC, so we should have had way more, but no, you can only get a certain number of foods or drinks with WIC, but with everything else, it was pretty much fair game.

When it came to Christmas, my brothers and I never expected anything. When we did, it was from other families, not parents. When my parents did get us things, each kid might get two gifts if we were lucky.

However, we would have to share the last one.

We were taught that with whatever we got, we had to share it, but I was okay with that because all I ever did was share or give something of mine away.

One Christmas, my biological parents got me a 14k gold pendant necklace. To this day, I wonder how they could afford it or what they had to do to get it.

I still have it, but I do not wear it.

The only time we did have a Christmas was when my aunt, uncle, grandparents, and Angel Tree places tried to give it to us. No matter how far away they were, they still provided us with what we needed and a little extra to play with. We would always get one pair of shoes from them, a few outfits, and a toy or two for us older kids and the others.

Treating us equally is what they wanted to do so no one was left behind. We always believed our aunt, uncle, and grandparents would get us something every Christmas. When their money was tight, they still managed to bring a smile to our faces, even if the gifts were only clothes. We would be happy with anything we got because we got almost nothing from our real parents.

On some Christmas mornings, we would go to my grandfather's house and find a large Christmas tree with sparkly lights, ornaments, and decorations. There were even presents underneath for all of us kids to open.

We felt like we were actual children during those times, but certainly not because of my parents.

My Aunt Teresa would come down and visit a few times, and each time she did, I would love it.

She was always calm and would bring her youngest so I would have a girl with whom to interact.

I am not sure if she knew everything that was going on with us, but she had an idea that anytime someone intervened, they would be cut out of our lives, or my biological parents would move away. I saw her almost every other year when she lived in New York, but she eventually stopped because my parents moved.

Another family member who made things fun or would take me on camping trips or just to his house to spend the night and hang with my cousin would be my great Uncle Charles. He was one of the few men I could trust and feel safe with in my young life. He used to drive what I called a '70s van with spinning chairs and velvet-like seats. At his house, he had a bearded dragon that was crazy to hold but cool to watch.

My brother Shawn and I often had to play the parent roles to my four baby brothers. I was a mother figure to them because I always ensured they had what they needed, especially regarding food and clothes.

If Shawn or I got some extra money, his would be for things he and I needed, and mine would be for the younger ones. If it weren't for Shawn and me, my little brothers would not have had the life they did.

One time, Shawn had this conversation.

"Sis, do you remember when we got some money that you always put some of it away for an emergency?"

"Sure, I remember doing that. I would always spend whatever extra money I had on the boys."

"Yes, Ally, anywhere from one dollar to five dollars You used to put it in that Pokémon ball we had."

"I know, but it disappeared. I always thought that maybe it was accidentally packed away somewhere."

"No, sis, that bitch of an egg donor and ass of a sperm donor found where you had it hidden."

"Please don't tell me what they did with that money because I think I already know."

"Our sperm donor didn't want to touch it… but she told him it was okay, so he did."

"How do you know this, Shawn?"

"I saw you hide it and wanted to help you out, so as I went to the spot to put some money in it, I saw Mom there. She had opened it and was counting the money."

"Well, I don't remember how much was in there, but it must have been close to two hundred dollars." "

No, Sis, you had about five hundred dollars."

"Wow, I can't believe she'd do something like that. She makes so much money, so why go for mine?"

"Ally, it's okay. Remember, money is just money. What's important is the relationship you have with us."

♥ ♥ ♥ ♥ ♥

From the ages of 5 to 9, while we lived in Arizona, I always dreamed of what life was like in others' houses.

Those years were crucial to my childhood and my upbringing. My little self was so bubbly despite being abused. I loved being outside, playing with Barbies when I had some, or watching TV… but that changed when one particular family member started coming around and hanging out more than he should.

He paid extra attention to me and showed it in ways that were not acceptable. Not understanding what he was doing was wrong because it was happening in my home, and since other men were also doing similar stuff, I thought it was okay in the beginning.

One of the times I remember Tony touching me was when we were living in a mobile home park in Tucson. I was in the bed that I shared with my younger siblings. The bedroom was at the other end of the trailer. He came and laid next to me under the covers and quickly slid his hand in between my shorts.

It hurt, so I said, "I don't like that; it hurts."

He said, "Sush, it will be okay," and then covered my mouth. I was wearing my Barbie shirt, which had a stain on the side and a rip on the sleeve, and pink ruffle shorts with white underwear and flowers.

After he finished touching me with his hand, he said, "It won't happen again, but don't tell anyone."

Well, he lied about that because each time he got another chance to molest me, he would.

I tried to tell my real mom about it, but she just said, "Hey, it happens in families," making it seem normal.

There were multiple times that he did what he did, but the last time he did anything to me was right before I turned nine when we moved to another trailer. Again, I was sharing a room with my younger siblings, as most places we lived in had only one or two bedrooms.

This time, the room I was in had a bathroom.

We still had roaches, cats, and dogs everywhere, but as much as all that grossed me out, what he did to me changed my view on life at such an early age.

I washed my hands after using the restroom and started to change because I was planning to shower.

I couldn't lock the door because it was broken, and I was wearing only my shirt when he walked in.

When he started touching me, I cried and told him it hurt too much. I said if he loved me, he would not do it.

I believe he was under the influence, which does not give him an excuse, but he grabbed me, sat me on the counter, and tried to penetrate me.

When that didn't work, he grabbed me by my face and proceeded to engage in oral sex, forcing himself into my mouth. When he was done with me, he had me drink Sprite to wash the taste out of my mouth.

After this occurrence, I heard about people killing themselves and also saw it in movies. After everything that had happened with my uncle, I was so depressed that I attempted suicide for the first time.

I found my father's razor blade and tried to slit my wrists. I remember it hurting at first, but then everything calmed down. What brought me out of it was my little brother walking into the bathroom and hugging me.

He said, "I love you."

I had only cut myself a little, so I stopped and went to a neighbor who was a nurse and got cleaned up before my real mom came back from one of her binges.

My aunt, uncle, and even my grandparents fought with my parents numerous times to get us kids out of the house. They wanted to have custody but never got us. Each time they tried, we were taken to a foster home, or our parents cleaned up their act just long enough to have us released back into their custody.

As soon as they got us back from the multiple foster homes, they would return to their idiotic habits of drug addiction and sex binges.

Once, our aunt and uncle actually had a chance to take Shawn and me, being the two oldest, but I told the police I wanted to stay, maybe because I could not leave the little ones in the same predicament and thought my older brother and I could save them.

I quickly regretted that horrible decision after the day our real father brutally beat my brother, and I was dragged across the yard by my hair while my real mom slapped me in the face several times.

Sometimes, my real mother would say she was a nurse, but I was young and naïve, so I didn't know what the powder on the table in the kitchen actually was.

If I had a stomachache, she would take some of the powder and mix it with water, then put it in a syringe and inject it into my ankle. I was not fond of needles.

Within minutes, I went from having a stomachache to where my body felt like it was burning all over.

The first time this happened, I felt terrified.

She said, "Oh, don't worry, you will eventually go to sleep and wake up feeling better."

I did fall asleep, but as soon as I woke up, I began throwing up. She finally gave me Gatorade and some crackers, and I felt better, but anytime I was sick, she would give me that syringe.

Over time, I became malnourished.

I did not think my father knew everything until I told him one day, "Mommy keeps giving me a syringe with white stuff in it." Again, he yelled at her, and some violence happened. After that, she never did it again.

Shawn and my father would get physical quite often. A vivid time was when we were living in the trailer park on Benson Ave. I do not remember what it was about exactly, but my father grabbed Shawn by the hair and pulled it so hard it took a chunk of hair out. Shawn then took a screwdriver and stabbed our father in the leg, puncturing the skin and causing him to bleed.

The commotion became so unbelievably crazy my mother screamed, alerting the neighbors, who called the police. Our father was arrested and spent a couple of days in jail, so we stayed with my grandmother.

When it came to education, I surprisingly did well when I was younger. I never got anything lower than a 'B,' and I actually had to teach myself.

My real mom never finished high school.

She dropped out in her sophomore year, and my dad finished high school. They taught me how to solve some problems in math and reading, but after third grade, I'm not sure if it was because they forgot or did not know how, but from then on, I was on my own. It was the same with my older brother; although he was in special education classes at times, he still had to self-educate.

My brother also helped me with math because he was terrific at it. I made student of the month almost every month, with perfect attendance, maybe twice a year because of all the moving and family situations.

Being in school was my escape from my mother and father. I did whatever it took to ensure I was in school because, for those few hours, I had what I considered freedom and could be a child.

I had to do a lot of work, but it was almost fun.

I did not have someone pulling my hair if I did not finish, getting slapped in the face, or kicked in the stomach if it wasn't correct. I had adult teachers who helped and pushed me only because they saw the potential.

I felt safe, although I still got bullied every week for the clothes I wore, for my hair not always washed, and sometimes for not being able to shower, or for my speech impediment and stutter, but that was nothing to what I endured at home and made me feel less than.

I became close to a few people, and even now, we're still friends. Casey, Aimee, Bethany, and a few others were girls who not only befriended me but helped me if I needed clothes or spare change for lunch, and Casey and Aimee's mom were godsends for the times I stayed over at their house to get away.

My parents uniquely disciplined each of the kids.

Since I was the only girl, I did not get disciplined the way you would think. My older brother got it worse.

He took a lot of beatings for the rest of us.

My little brothers were still slapped, punched, and kicked at times, as was I. We were all abused.

So many of the memories I have of getting hit are from stepping in front of my little brothers to prevent them from getting hit, but as much as my brothers and I were abused, we grew up with a strong bond. However, we were broken inside. The abuse seemed to worsen as we got older, and my parents became addicts.

The bruises and bloody noses were constant, and each time someone asked me about it, I would just say, "I have four brothers, and we like to play hard."

Some of the conversations I had with people when they saw the marks were very different. One day, my friend and I talked, and she was worried.

"Ally, you and your brothers must get out of there."

"I know we need to, but I'm afraid the situation will worsen if we leave. I never want to be placed in another stranger's home again."

"You need help, and I want to help you."

"I'm okay, but thank you for the offer," I told her.

I knew that I was strong enough to pull through and care for myself and my brothers.

Some people believed it. My friends who had seen some of it firsthand did not ever say anything. When they did say something, I was comforted but denied it and kept with the same story about my brothers and me.

As time passed by and the days seemed to be slower and more challenging, my brothers and I waited for the day when all this misery would end and we would be able to live a better life than we lived.

My older brother and I got a break when we visited our aunt and uncle because, at least there, we got fed, were given nice clothes, got our teeth brushed, could wash our hair, and felt healthy.

Shawn and I were so unfortunate to have lived the lifestyle we had because we never had the childhood we should've had. We had been in and out of foster homes from the time I can remember when I started talking.

All my other siblings were the same way.

Initially, staying in foster homes didn't feel much different from just visiting someone for a while. Still, as I got older, I felt sad being separated from my family, even though we were safer. We should have been on a reality TV show with everything going on.

Learning I was going to move to another state with my biological family seemed like a promising idea, but right before that, when I was nine years old, I did not think anything could get worse than what my uncle had already done, but I was wrong.

I was living on Benson Ave. by the sheriff's station when my innocence was completely and unimaginably stolen from me. This forever scared me and, to this day, still gives me nightmares.

Living with this and my parents knowing made me feel like they did not care about me whatsoever.

All I wanted was to move and get away from that nightmare, the childhood memories that broke me, and the suffering we all endured in so many different ways.

Part Two: What Finally Broke Me

March 2003:

On a pleasant Tuesday afternoon, I knew I had to go with my real mother so she could have sex with some stranger in exchange for drugs and money. We walked up to the room two doors down from where we lived.

It was like everything was planned.

A little table with crayons and a coloring book sat in a dark corner. She told me to go over there to color and stay out of the bedroom where they were going. As the minutes passed, I heard some loud noises. I was afraid to go in, but then I heard my mom scream. I ran in as fast as I could, thinking she was hurt. What I saw was her and a dark-skinned guy with needles in their arms.

Not knowing what was happening, I went up to help my mom. The guy grabbed my head, threw me against the wall, and busted my lip. I crawled to the bed crying, wondering why my mother did nothing to protect me, but all she did was smile as if she wasn't entirely there; I closed my eyes and hoped it would all stop.

I don't know how much time passed, but at some point, I must have passed out from the shock.

I recall that she was acting extremely weird.

She was talking gibberish and snorting some sort of white powder while sitting on a table.

The guy flipped me over and started touching me.

I tried scratching, kicking, and even biting him to get off of me, but being only about seventy pounds with a two-hundred-pound man on top wasn't helping.

His disgusting, big, wet lips were all over my body.

My crying red eyes met the drug-addicted eyes of a demon, but he kept on going. The worst part came when he removed my blue jean skirt and Barney panties.

I was in agony as something large and strange began to intrude into my body. I was in pain, embarrassed, and angry. As he continued, I looked at my mother, who just smiled as she did before, still not there.

I closed my eyes, hoping it would soon end.

Again, I don't remember how much time passed, but I sat up as soon as he got off of me, still not realizing what had just happened.

The first thing I saw was a pool of blood on the bed.

I could see my mom and the demon, who were both naked in the living room, about to have sex. As I reached down to feel my body, I realized that I was also nude, and there was blood in the downstairs department.

Suddenly, it all hit me!! There's no way to describe how I felt other than devastated, so I dressed and sat on the edge of the bed until we finally went home.

My mother was all doped up and had no clue what happened to me. My father never knew because I didn't tell him. A few days later, I saw a doctor and told him what had happened, so he did an exam, and he told my parents, but they were clueless about what happened.

My father then asked me about it, but the man was already gone by then.

Once my dad had heard what happened to me, I also told him about the family member, so he and the family member got into a fight. My mom blamed me for the family member getting hurt despite what he did to me.

When she lashed out, I ran behind a dresser that had a toolbox on top. She tried to push the dresser on top of me, but instead, the toolbox fell onto my face, cutting my cheek open.

Again, the neighbors heard the commotion, called the police, and my parents were issued a warrant.

Adding to that, we had to leave.

To this day, my real mom still denies it happened and calls me a liar, probably because she feels guilty, or maybe it's because she does not remember.

After this incident, with my cuts still not fully healed from trying to take my life the first time, I tried again on my left wrist but barely did a thing. I stopped because I was afraid if I left, what would happen to my brothers?

One time, Child Protective Services got involved in something unrelated. I was signed up to receive abuse counseling from my POS mother. I thought that talking to someone about everything that happened would make me feel safer or better, but I was wrong.

As I walked into the room, I saw two adults: a tall Hispanic male with dark hair who looked like he was in his mid-thirties and a tall white woman with dark hair who looked in her early to mid-thirties. They asked me if I wanted to sit down, which I did without knowing what to expect or do.

They began asking me questions about the incidents that happened. I told them about my uncle and the man that raped me, thinking that telling them would help me.

They asked me if I had dressed a certain way and why I chose to go with my mother on the day of the rape.

I was 10 years old. I told them, "Mommy always dressed me when we would go to these guys' places, and on that specific day, she dressed me in smaller clothes."

I did not know what the words 'provocative, slut, or demeaning' meant until the man said, "You chose to go with your mom and dress provocatively. Why didn't you stay home, go to the house your younger siblings were at, or go to school?"

He made me feel it was my fault, so I started crying and told him the truth, "I'm too little to stay home alone.

If I did, a man would come to the house while mommy was out, and I didn't like what he did."

The woman changed the subject and went to the topic of my uncle and said, "Why did you let him do it so long?" Did you not tell anyone?"

I cried even more and told her, "I did, but no one believed me, and my mother told me it's normal because it happens in families."

I was scared of being in there alone and shouldn't have been alone in the first place.

At the end of that so-called counseling meeting, they told me, "It's your fault it happened because of how you were dressed and didn't speak up or say no."

Hearing those words made me realize that no one in this world would ever help me. I was going to live this life until I ended up dead or taken away for good.

Part Three: The Tipping Point

Moving to another state felt like starting a new life, but 'moving on' in my family's case just meant they were running away again. Boy was I wrong!

The sign said, 'Welcome to New Mexico,' which was our destination, but it was there where the abuse, neglect, and use of drugs only heightened.

School was probably the only opportunity to keep us kids going and smiling because it was when we were not home. I was in New Mexico from fifth to seventh grade. At the beginning of our stay there, it was the regular day at home. The fighting, drugs, and abuse were normal. When we were living in one of the many hotels, my biological father was at work, and it was just me and my younger siblings; my older brother was already gone.

My little brother Dyson had walked out the door as I attended to the baby, and my biological mother was in the kitchen getting a drink. We got a knock at the door, and there were two police officers, a white male and a black male. They asked us all to step outside, and when I saw my brother Dyson, I knew something was wrong.

They took my biological mother to the side, but the rest of us stayed where we were.

I was alone in the corner of the stairwell with the rest of my younger brothers. My baby brother started to scream, so I tried to console him, but he wanted Mom.

I remember her telling the officer, "Let me grab my baby, please." As she turned to walk back inside, the officer grabbed her arm and said she couldn't leave.

"I'm just getting my baby," she replied.

He grabbed her again and shoved her to the ground with his leg on her upper back. As the other officer was cuffing her, I started crying and screaming because my biological mother was getting hurt. I put my little brother in his crib, called my father, told him what was happening, and told my other brothers, "It's okay."

I went outside and told the officers to stop hurting my mom and grabbed the black officer's arm to get him off my mother by scratching his arm; he then pushed me against the wall and put cuffs on me for attacking an officer and set me in the back of the squad car.

My mom was picked up still in cuffs and set down next to my brothers; then my father pulled up.

At just eleven years old, there I was, sobbing in the back seat of a police car and very scared. Whatever my father said, my mom's handcuffs were removed. I was also uncuffed and told to go upstairs with the rest of my brothers. It was a horrible experience. As abused as it had been living at home, the police were worse.

♥ ♥ ♥ ♥ ♥

At the beginning of seventh grade, my life began to change. Stephen, the oldest brother of the four youngest, nearly died because my real father and mother mixed his cystic fibrosis medication with alcohol.

"How stupid could they be," I kept saying.

After it happened a second time to him, they were so messed up he had been taken away.

A month later, the rest of us were also removed.

It was so sad because we had finally moved into an actual house with doors, no broken windows, functional bathrooms, a backyard, and where I had a private room. We had only been in this place for maybe a week.

I remember my real mom walking me to the bus stop that morning with my brothers, and I said to her, "Mom, I have a bad feeling about today. I don't think I should go to school." She responded, "Baby girl, it will be okay. We will all see you when you get home."

I was right. Getting off that bus and walking up to my house, seeing what I saw, I thought maybe I was dreaming, but no, I was not.

It was in the middle of August, on a bright sunny day after school, the last day my family would ever be together. As I walked down the sidewalk, I saw two police cars: a forensics car and a news vehicle, and I was thinking, "Maybe they are there for another house."

I was certain there must have been a murder or something, not realizing they were actually at my home. As I got closer, my younger brothers Dyson and Casper, ages three and five, came running up to me and said, "Mommy and Daddy got arrested."

As soon as I heard that, I ran with them inside to find my ten-month-old brother in the arms of our case worker and everyone in the house but my parents.

I asked, "Why is this happening? What is going on?"

"You guys are going to be placed in a foster home, and your parents will be in jail." replied the caseworker.

I started getting mad and made it evident that I did not want to be split up from my babies because they meant so much to me, but I was told it wouldn't happen.

Gathering some belongings for me and my brothers, we exited the house. The boys got in a Child Protective Services car, and they put me in the back of a police car.

We drove to the station, not knowing why.

Several hours later, they finally told me that my real parents had been arrested for the previous incidents with my brother Steven, who had nearly died, and now my parents were both facing warrants for physical, mental, and sexual abuse.

After my older brother had been taken away a month earlier and asked to be removed, I felt they would be in trouble, but I was never expecting it to happen like that.

Separating my little brothers and me into rooms at the station only made my attitude more intense. I mean, they put me in an interrogation room and asked me questions. I was twelve years old and knew right from wrong, but come on, guys, something traumatic had just happened. After an hour of questioning, someone told us that we were going to a foster home and would have to be separated.

My baby brother Wally and I were in one home, and the other two, Dyson and Casper, went together. Before this, when my little brothers heard they were getting separated from me, they started crying, saying, "Sissy, Sissy, do not leave us. We love you, stay, stay."

Thinking of that now makes me break down because of the look on their faces. Their watery eyes with their pushed-out bottom lips, grabbing my hands to hold them and never letting go would make you melt with tears.

As we were getting ready to go our separate ways, my little brothers came up to me and hugged me, saying, "We love you, Sissy, and always will. We want us to be together again soon."

Realizing that they may not know everything and that this would be the last time we'd be together as a family, I simply smiled and said, "No matter how far apart we are from one another, whatever the situation, I'll always find time to be with you guys."

After we parted ways and went to our different homes, I wondered how long I'd be in this home this time and what the outcome would be.

♥ ♥ ♥ ♥ ♥

Wally and I stayed in this foster home for the entire seventh grade, and when May came along, my older brother and I went to live with my aunt and uncle back in Arizona, which was a tough decision, not only for myself but for my aunt and uncle as well. I did not want to be even further from my brothers than I was, nor did my older brother. My aunt and uncle wanted to take us all but could not do so under the state guidelines.

Leaving my baby brothers crushed me because they thought it was going to be a typical Friday when we would all meet up and hang out, but it would be the last.

It was on Good Friday in May. I woke up, smelling the fresh air, looking out the window of my foster home into the street where neighbors I once befriended and kids I used to play with, knowing it would be the last.

I had put on my Lisa Frank outfit, which consisted of a top, skirt, and sandals, and kept my hair down.

I dressed my baby brother in a blue and green striped Elmo shirt and blue jean shorts with black tennis shoes with his hair combed to the side.

Sitting in the car going down the streets with my stuff packed in the back, I knew it would be the start of my new life, but in the back of my head, I knew it would not be over for the younger ones.

After getting to Child Protective Services, I stepped out of the big white car and looked at all my brothers with my baby brother on my hip. I ran to them and hugged them like I had not seen them in years. My older brother hugged us, and we proceeded with our visit.

We played some games like tic-tac-toe, had lunch together, laughed, and had fun. Time went so slowly, but it was a good slow time for this situation.

When I saw my aunt and uncle, it was like a heavy toolbox being lifted off my chest. I was getting set free. We all interacted, and we left when it was time to go.

The boys thought we would be gone for the summer, but that was not the case.

One year went by. I was in the eighth grade, and things were going smoothly while living with my aunt and uncle. I was still getting to call my brothers every week and visit once a month.

During that year, I met my current best friend/sister, Lynette. We hit it off so fast and were inseparable until she had to move into high school.

It was not until my first year in high school and my brother's Junior year that we got adopted.

The court hearing was pretty scary, but it was an awesome experience. My biological mother showed up because, by now, she had been released from jail, but my father was only able to talk by telephone.

They agreed to share their rights with me and my older brother so we could live. Signing my new name relieved me of the name I used to have.

I began to feel like a new person.

When I arrived, I was a preteen.

I finally started living my childhood.

My room was filled with Tinker Bell everywhere: comfort, lamps, and dresses. I even had a canopy that was pink over my bed. As I became a teenager, I started living my preteen years, so you get the picture.

However, the funny part is that even though I was in a better living environment, I was still trying to find myself and figure out who I was and wanted to become in my later years.

Throughout high school, I lived a sheltered life, mostly because even though I was nice and bubbly, I was still timid in many ways. My parents played a role in it because I was never allowed to go to anyone's house, let alone spend the night because of my young childhood, which I was okay with for some time until I got older. I would do sports, and there would be outings with the team I wanted to do, such as sleepovers with girls from cheer and dance. Sometimes, I was scared to participate, but only because I feared something happening to me again and not knowing how to take it.

I used to tell my adoptive parents things even when I didn't need to, but I wanted to because I believed that I would be okay as long as they knew.

My adoptive parents were better than my biological parents, but they still had toxic traits, such as narcissism, and abuse of one another, and had to be in control.

I did not go to my first 'party' until I was eighteen, which was a Halloween party. I was a little worried because I wasn't sure what to expect from a party other than what I had seen in movies or been told, although it's not always relatable.

I graduated in 2011 amongst my peers.

My family was there: my parents, my grandparents, grandma Louise, sister, brother and nephew.

♥ ♥ ♥ ♥ ♥

My adoptive dad had his controlling moments, not just over my adoptive mom but over us kids as well.

To an extent, I felt like he was doing it to protect us, but as a child/teenager, you feel like you have no life.

He and my adoptive mom were very abusive to one another, which my brother and I were not expecting.

I had endured and seen so much abuse as a young child that I did not want to experience it again, but I did.

Everyone has their side in every story, but as a child, you see more than what they say.

I remember a time when my brother and I had gotten home and were walking to the backdoor to unload our stuff. We turned the corner, and my adoptive dad shoved my mom up against the back of the truck they had and had his arm over her throat. She punched him to get out of it, and I immediately ran inside to tell Shawn.

He went out there, acted like he didn't know, and asked, "What was for dinner?" They both came inside like nothing happened, but I told my dad I saw him hit Mom. He told me, "You saw nothing."

I then told my mom I had seen what dad did, and she told me she was okay and to leave it alone.

My adoptive parents were overprotective at times, and again, I understood why to an extent, but because I did not go out much, I rebelled a little.

What kid doesn't do that?

Honestly? What I mean by rebel is I experienced weed, went to a few parties, and drank, but only once because I was afraid. They knew some details but not all because I realized I was old enough to make my own decisions and suffer consequences if needed.

However, I did not know that they would get so mad when they found out months later where I was.

Talk about the craziness that ensued.

I did not know who I was or understood myself until right around my freshman year in college.

There, I discovered that I was not only someone but also me, Ally, the girl who had come from so little and expected nothing but had come a long way.

♥ ♥ ♥ ♥ ♥

My older brother and I did great in school. We both graduated and are now living different lives.

He will be getting married and has two lovely kids, Derek who is three, and little Serenity, who is six months, will be seven in just a few months.

His soon-to-be wife is his high school sweetheart Melody. They have their own place, and he has a job.

We still have contact with our siblings occasionally, but not our parents.

I am a junior in college pursuing the prerequisites for my Nursing degree with the scholarship I earned from the Bruce T. Halle Foundation. The scholarship was offered to seven students through Discount Tire.

I had to write three essays, two being five hundred words and the other being one thousand, get letters of recommendation, and then write why I deserve it.

I bought a car when I was eighteen, got my braces off, and started wearing glasses.

Soon after that, I met a sweet guy who got me a promise ring. It was my first real relationship. We loved each other as we did a lot of firsts together, but not all.

I traveled with him for a while. He took me to Ohio, where he was from, to meet his family. He was stationed here for the military in the Air Force.

Although our relationship didn't work out, I had some experiences with him that molded me for my next relationship. Little did I know that I would go on a date and get raped just months later.

Yes, I went on a date with a guy I had known for only a short while and went to dinner, a movie, and a party at his house. I knew that going to a new guy's house was not always wise, but I figured it was fine as there were multiple people. I drove my car, thinking I could leave if I wanted. I knew about date rape drugs but never thought it would be like that.

I had a shot and one punch drink that tasted funky, but I thought it was a mixture of drinks.

I drank half of it before I started feeling sick, and it's still foggy to this day. I remember dancing and the guy saying, "Lay down." There was a bed. I must have passed out for what felt like forever, but I woke up to him standing naked, taking something off and saying,

"Oh shit, it broke." I was trying to understand what had happened, but I was sleepy. I heard a door close, and he left. After I awoke, I was still loopy but went home.

I knew what happened after I came home that night;

I told my mom, and she said she would go with me to get tested and everything because I was scared, and she did not want me to go alone. That following day, I got up and did everything on my own as my mom did not go with me. I later found out I did get an STI but was treated for it. During the treatment, my mom, whom I thought would help me through this, treated me like I was disease-ridden. She would not drink after me or hug me and said, "I don't want to get it; I can't get sick."

I said, "Mom, it doesn't work like that." Eventually, once she knew it was clear, she looked past it.

He did get arrested but only served 6 months in jail.

A year later, I went to Disneyland for the first time with my parents, sister, and grandpa. I was nineteen.

That was exciting for me.

Vacations did not happen when I lived with my real parents, but with my adoptive parents, I did things from going to SeaWorld, learning how to surf, or trying the beach and Oregon to meet my dad's mom, who is an absolute sweetheart, Chery, a woman who opened her arms to my brother and me with no hesitation and quickly became known as Grammie. I always had a wonderful time with Grammie Chery.

I was hesitant about what would be next in my life. Throughout this, I met a wonderful girl named Aurora.

We had gone to high school together in our senior year but hung out with different people. We instantly got close as we were both going through the breakups of our then-boyfriend's freshman year in college. I was still feeling down but knew I needed to stay around.

One of my relationships that became stronger was with my sister, who is actually my cousin, but I have been with her since she was four months old, and all she has ever known is that I am Sissy, and Shawn is Bubby.

As she got older, she knew she did not come out of my mom's belly… but we were siblings. She looked up to me and wanted to be like me. She wanted to do everything I did as well, from dancing, cheering, and even kickboxing to anything. Our age gap is about thirteen years, but we are so close that sometimes I'd forget she was younger, and I would tell her secrets that she may not understand… but being able to say it was awesome.

She was my best friend, a mini-me, and I loved her.

As for my other brothers, they have all been adopted and have a loving life.

My brother Steven is living in Ohio because the family he lives with can afford his medical needs for Cystic Fibrosis. Dyson is in New Mexico with a family who wants him to have zero contact with the rest of us for a reason I do not know. Casper and Wally are with a lovely couple in their sixties in New Mexico.

Steven's world is wrapped around girls because he is sixteen and about to be seventeen. I have no idea how Dyson is doing except what I am told. Casper is doing good in school but not as good as he should. He is in fifth grade. Wally is smart and loves to play instruments and is only in third grade but was allowed to play in the band, which is only for fifth graders and up.

We try to visit each other at least once a year.

I know that if I were to go and be released back to my biological parents, I sure would not be where I am today. I would have been pregnant at least twice, on drugs, and never finished high school. I say that with complete animosity against my parents because they should have known better and been more grown up.

All of my brothers probably would have been in fights and in and out of the juvenile system.

Shawn and I agreed to call our adoptive parents Mom and Dad as soon as we got adopted, but it took us some time to get used to it because it was a little weird at first, but after a while, it felt right.

They will always be our parents no matter what, and that is how we introduce them. We chose them to be our heroes because they did not physically have us but took us in and raised my brother and me as their own.

Those who adopt us are even stronger because the love is deeper than any love I can compare it to.

Without these two, I would probably be in a ditch somewhere on drugs, and my brother would be in jail for drugs or violence.

My dad did love us and showed us love despite his anger. My grandfather also showed us love and was there for every event. My dad taught us how to play sports, drive (scary a little bit), and work on a car.

My dad did his best to show up to every event. He was a hard worker. My mom made sure we had food, would cook for us, and showed us how to cook certain things, which was funny. She showed me how to do my hair or did it for me since I did not know how.

My grandma taught me how to sew and iron and even told me what a hot totty was. She and my mom would do my hair when I was a child, put me in cute outfits, and take me shopping, except I dressed myself.

My grandfather and his wife Louise (my other grandma) would ask me to work for them to make some extra money during the summers because I wanted to have some shopping money.

Then we'd go to the VFW to get my Shirley Temple and play some games. It was always fun with them.

We spent Thanksgiving and Christmas together, and it was always a family event. My grandfather would dress up as Santa some years, and I thought that was the coolest thing as I had never experienced Santa in my life, let alone an experience like that. Throughout all this, probably wondering if I had done something to clear my mind or let out some anger, and I did.

I had taken a fitness class with an instructor who kept me on my toes with exercises from Yoga, cardio, conditioning, and more, which helped me emotionally.

This was also a dark time for me, though, because even though I had been through worse, I started feeling depressed, and each time I did, I felt like not being here anymore and tried to take my life. I didn't want to die, so I did what I could to feel alive and keep going, such as working out. I was vulnerable and felt like I was only an object, especially to guys, so I used my body for that specific reason. I never felt needed for love, just lust or sex. No, I did not sleep around, but I was numb to a lot of it after so many years of abuse from someone who said they cared and men coming and going as a child, which was still in my brain. I couldn't tell my parents or really anyone because of how I was treated when I got the STI and them being part of the problem.

I felt alone.

I had people around me, but I still felt alone.

I silently fought inside my brain more times than I could count as to what was going on with my life.

I needed to change and know my worth. So, I just smiled and went on like I always did, even though I was still struggling and numb.

I had people who looked up to me and had my brothers and little sister to be here for.

Through all this silence, I continued to move on with a smile even through the toughest, darkest, and scariest times, hoping something stronger, lighter, and happier would someday happen.

It may take time, but it will; you just have to believe.

Those of you who do not think there is light at the end of the tunnel, keep your eyes open, your head up, and always smile no matter what.

Eventually, I grew out of the hole into a beautiful, loved, and cherished, yet still a little broken flower.

Part Four: Healing Begins

I changed my college major several times over the next two years, only to circle back to the beginning.

When I was taking classes in nursing school and had to write a paper for my English class as a final project, I chose my childhood.

During my early years in college, a lovely couple, the Parkers, who were both my professors and helped me through so much, even visiting me in the hospital when I had seizures. They became family instantly, like parents, and told others, "This is our other daughter."

I received a degree in liberal arts while waiting to get into Nursing school. I went on a few more vacations with my parents, sister, and grandma during this time.

I got to go to Universal for the first time, which was just as fun as Disneyland, if not better.

In fact, I experienced many things as a young adult that most people experienced as children.

Through college, I worked at Starbucks and learned everything anyone would want to know about coffee; plus, I met some awesome people along the way and have remained good friends with Helena and Harmony, both amazing women.

As each year passed, I continued to think about my childhood and where I am now. I had gone to a couple of concerts, from "Tool" to "Flo Rida" to "Trey Songs," thanks to my girl Aurora. We did a lot together.

Considering my upbringing, I was living my life as best as I could.

Each year, I had contact with my two younger brothers and would see them when they visited. It was always a great feeling to have that connection with them.

Also, around this time, I knew where my real parents were but did not want to communicate with them, as the last time I talked to my real mom when I was thirteen, she called me a "lying bitch." She did not like it when I told her how she let things happen to me and that she chose her fix over us. My real dad was still in prison at this point. He had been in and out since we were taken.

I did write to him while he was in prison and learned some things I did not need to know, but towards the end of those letters, he apologized for the childhood my brother and I had and did not deserve. He apologized for not being able to do more but also admitted it had a lot to do with drugs. I eventually stopped replying as it was getting too much for me and emotional.

As for my real mom, she was residing in Texas.

She was married again and had another little boy I still have yet to meet because I don't want to see her.

It was important to focus on my future without being distracted. It had taken almost a year to get over my ex. I didn't want to endure any more trauma or drama.

I had taken a psychology class and realized that the abuse I suffered as a child was not over and that I was still experiencing it differently from my family.

♥ ♥ ♥ ♥ ♥

By March of 2015, life was feeling good.

I started talking to Johnny, an awesome older man with two children. He changed my perspective on life and men in general. I was at the point where guys only viewed me as an object and had used me my whole life, but Johnny made me feel good about myself.

He took his time and listened to me.

It was not 100% great only because of the situation.

Everything was good until his baby mama found out and made everything so hard.

She kept threatening to tell my parents.

Mind you, I was 22 years old, but my parents were not like that when I was a kid, or so I thought.

His baby mama stalked me at school and work and had people threaten to beat me up, even kill me if I kept seeing him. They had never married and were not even together when he and I got together.

She was horrible.

With all of this going on, Melody, my sister-in-law, had just given birth to my nephew Landon.

Johnny and I tried to make things easy on ourselves because we wanted to stay together. A few months later, we told each other we loved one another.

It was not until October 2015 that his baby mama decided to call my dad to tell him about us.

Now, you're probably thinking, "You're an adult; what does it matter who you're with or not, let alone to your parents."

That's correct; it should not have mattered, but it did because this older gentleman worked alongside my dad, which is how we ran into each other.

At the end of 2015, I had my first auto accident and totaled my car. Johnny had to change jobs because of our relationship, although it did not affect his job.

To top it off, I was helping take care of Aurora, who was sick and needed help, and I knew she needed me.

♥ ♥ ♥ ♥ ♥

From the very beginning, my parents, especially my mom, always asked if I was dating. I did tell her I was seeing someone but never divulged who it was.

My dad found out first and was hurt by the lies from both of us because my dad thought he was a good friend.

As he put it, he felt betrayed and began to treat me a little differently, but once my mom found out, it was like seeing another side of her I had never seen before.

The first time, she was upset but then would call him and say, "I know you're a good person and will treat my daughter well; I just wish you had said something."

Two days later, she would call and say, "How could you do this to me? You have hurt me so bad."

Between the pressure of Johnnys baby mama and the shit she was doing to me, and my parent's attitude towards me, I tried to take my life once again.

This time, I took a bunch of pills but just got sick.

My dad found me in the bathroom and told me that no matter how he felt about my life, my life was worth something, and he loved me.

After that, I wanted to try to please everyone.

The Parkers were there for me during this and never judged me, but only because they were worried for me as I was getting micromanaged by the baby mama and how my parents were treating me.

I acted like I broke up with him because I had tried multiple times but could never do it.

My parents behaved well for the next six months because they were under the impression I was single.

In July 2016, I was dog-sitting for Aurora, and one night, I went to my boyfriend's house, not knowing my dad would swing by from his bike ride to check on me. Well, my car was there, but I was not.

He called me, and I told him I was not there and had to be picked up, so he began to get worried and angry.

Johnny drove me to the corner of where the house was, then I walked, and my dad picked me up.

We returned to the house, and he asked a few times after arguing before finally admitting that I was with Johnny and still saw him. The first time he found out, he had the same look on his face.

He said, "I knew it but hoped it was untrue."

He said it was up to me to tell my mom this time, but before I told her, he demanded that I break up with Johnny since I was still living at home. I was in school and working, so it was either do as he said or move out.

I waited another couple of months before I finally decided to move out. Not only did I need to, but I also wanted to because it was the only way I could be with Johnny. My dad was unhappy with me moving but helped me move my things. My mom was super sad because she did not understand why I was leaving.

I moved in with Aurora later in 2016.

During this move, I worked at a smoothie shop as a barista called Planet Smoothie. I loved it there.

It was by far one of my favorite jobs.

I met some great people there, such as the owner and her husband, who were brilliant, loving people; JD and his twin brothers; and Melissa and her daughter, Dior, whom I became close to, and we got tattoos together.

I stayed with my best friend for a few months but would still go to Johnnys house on the weekends.

Eventually, Johnny asked me to move in with him to save money for school. We both knew it was the right decision. Now, I am super grateful for my best friend Aurora, who opened her door to me, and I could never thank her enough.

I lived with Johnny during the new year of 2017.

We traveled together for the first time and went to New Mexico to see my little brothers.

With all this happening, Lynette asked to stay with Johnny, me, and her daughter Addison for a couple of days due to issues with her husband. Johnny's psycho baby mama was still doing her crazy stuff to where she started having my stepdaughter steal from me to get back at me but also to feel bad for her.

I was still talking to my parents even though they were upset with me. We still maintained a relationship for the rest of the year, if you can call it a relationship.

My mom sent hateful texts saying how disgusted she was with me being with Johnny. She said I hurt her more than my real mom could ever have done, which I could not believe, and that I was a horrible role model for my little sister. She even said it was my fault my grandfather got sick because "I cared more for my spick boyfriend than him."

My dad said he would beat Johnny up if he saw him again, and Johnny was a P.O.S. for doing what he did, not only to him but the family as well. He even said that Johnny was going to abuse me.

Talk about a lot of narcissism and manipulation.

I told both my parents, "I know what abuse is, and you are both one to talk."

They would say, "Wait until you're in an abusive situation. You will stay."

I was in an abusive relationship with my biological parents in more than one way, but abuse is still abuse no matter what. I would like to think I wouldn't stay, so forget that.

The relationship was toxic, and I dealt with it because I felt like they would get better. I was putting up with it until my world went from tolerable to heartache.

On November 17, 2017, Johnny proposed to me, which was the sweetest thing. With that next step came talking to his kids about how they felt about me.

Little Javier was just three years old when his dad and I were seeing each other, and Adrianna was twelve.

December 2017 was the last time I spoke with my family because they disapproved of my life choices.

I had yet to tell them I was freshly engaged.

On November 30, 2017, I had an intervention with my grandmother, grandfather, sister, and mom. All of them desperately wanted me to leave Johnny.

My grandfather said he still loved me and wanted to see me happy, but he didn't like how things turned out. He hugged me and said, "I love you, sweetheart."

I had no idea it would be the last time I'd ever see or hug my grandfather.

During this time, my brother Shawn and his family kept their distance because they did not want to have any issues, which really sucked because I missed my niece and nephews, and the bond I once had with my brother Shawn wasn't strong anymore.

On December 3, 2017, I went to my parents' house, thinking everything would be okay with them after that intervention. We ate food, and I helped them with the Christmas tree, which I do every year.

Once it was done, I was sitting there, and my mom called me into her room and gave me a globe.

I collected globes and shot glasses wherever I went.

The globe had the year 2017 with a horse in it.

Upon giving it to me, she says, "This is your gift because I won't see you for Christmas."

Hearing that hurt me because I loved my parents dearly and wanted their support at that time in my life, but I left that night with my heart broken, having tried my hardest to gain their support. That day would be the last day I'd see my mom for a few years.

I finished the end of 2017 celebrating with my now fiancé, Adrianna, and Javier.

We started looking at wedding venues as well.

Adriana was doing cheerleading in high school and volleyball, while Javier was learning so things from his favorite teacher, Mr. Stewart, to doing science projects.

Going into the beginning of 2018, it was an okay year. My dad still kept in contact with me so I could see how everyone was doing, and he just kept his distance.

Things were going as well as they could until the beginning of March. I got a few messages from my mom blaming me again for my grandfather being sick.

He ended up in the hospital and passed away on March 15, 2018. I only knew because my dad called me to tell me. That crushed me, and then having my mom who said some hateful things before blaming me again for his dying, which just about broke me, but I took some time to grieve. I wanted to go to the funeral and wait for some information, but I was not allowed to go and was banned from attending.

That's not even what completely broke me; it was the fact that my uncle was able to go (it was his father who passed), but I knew what kind of person he was and everything he did to me, knowing all that and still allowing him there over me.

Why, because I lied to you about who I was seeing?

But he had done the ultimate worst thing anyone could do, so I knew where I stood then.

♥ ♥ ♥ ♥ ♥

Two months after my grandfather passed, his wife Louise also passed, as well as my nana from my fiancé's side. Then, 2018 started off rocky and still is.

A few months after his funeral, my dad gave me some items of my grandfather's as I was not going to get anything. I'm forever grateful I got the items I did. He and my Grammie Chery had come to visit me while I was at work, and it felt so good to see her.

Oh, how much I love her.

By the summer of 2018, Johnny and I had sent out our save the dates and the invitations. Our wedding was planned for December 2018.

We were getting excited and had a venue picked out, the colors, and everything. Planning the wedding was stressful, but it was so much fun. Aurora and Lynette were to be my maids of honor, but Lynette had to step away from the wedding because of her husband at the time. I was sad, but I had to continue moving with my life, so instead, I asked Dior to take her place.

As we got closer to the wedding, I started having a bad feeling about this, and my feeling was right.

All I wanted was for both my parents to be at my wedding. I could not have my grandfather walk me down the aisle as he had passed, so I wanted my dad, but two days before the wedding, he told me, "I did not think you were going to go through with it, so I can no longer be a part of it."

After seeing my dad, I asked Mr Parker, my other father figure, if he would walk me down the aisle.

At first he was hesitant, but he said yes.

The wedding day came, and it was beautiful.

We got married at the Z Mansion.

When I first saw it, I fell in love with the stairwell, the lights, and everything. I was like a kid in a candy store. The colors were Fuchsia, teal, and silver.

This was the day every girl dreams of, or at least a lot of them do, so I was a ball of emotion.

My maid of honor was Aurora and Dior.

My bridesmaids were Adrianna, my cousin, and my sister-in-law Valerie. Johnny had his best man, his cousin, then his brother, Randy, his brother, Todd, and his best friends, Dave and Tom.

No one in my blood family came except my little brothers and their parents, whom I love as my own.

The Parkers were there to walk me down the aisle. Sitting in the front were some of my childhood friends and some close friends from school/college.

I walked down the stairs to meet Johnny to my song '*Crazy For You*' by Madonna.

I could see how happy he was as we walked back down the aisle as Mr. and Mrs. Abbot, this time to the song, '*I Was Made For Loving You*' by Kiss.

At the reception, our first dance was '*Back at One*' by Brian McKnight, which we both could relate to.

When I asked family members to participate, my parents persuaded some not to do so because a few of them didn't want issues, and the others sided with them.

I loved my wedding, and now I was married to my best friend and had two amazing stepkids, but my heart did not feel full. It was still wounded.

♥ ♥ ♥ ♥ ♥

It was 2019, a new year with another new name.

Up to this point, I'd had three identities.

It was two new beginnings, and I was overjoyed with the new family I had been welcomed into.

My husband's family was so nice. It was great to finally have some awesome people in my life. He had so many Tias and Tios and their families.

My father-in-law was so happy for us and opened his arms right away, alongside his wife.

His mom was also very accepting.

Valerie and her husband Francisco helped a lot with Javier, as did Todd and his wife.

Todd and Ashley have two kids, Luke and Lola.

Valerie and Francisco had Nelly.

My mother-in-law, Veronica, was helpful as well.

Randy and Jake were the brothers-in-law who were often funny. We went to an event every weekend, sometimes twice. Everyone says that Javier, my stepson, is good and so happy everywhere we go.

He says he loves me and has started calling me 'Mom number two,' as I have been raising him since he was four years old. I potty-trained him, and we did everything together. He loved the *Cars movie* and collects Hot Wheels Cars. I taught him many things as he got older and took care of him when he was sick and more.

Anytime he needed something, his dad and I would take care of him or get it because his mother was not living such a good lifestyle, neglecting his needs.

He is my son. Adrianna is my stepdaughter.

Together, they kept us on our toes.

She showed me things as a mom, and I taught her things that I was never taught. She experienced some things going back and forth between her mother and us, but in the end, it made her a better person.

As 2019 went on, I gained a good friend from nursing school, Keith, who attended my wedding.

I also started MA school at PMI, where I made some awesome friends and had great experiences.

That summer, my family and I went to New Mexico to see my little brothers. While we were there, I got to see my brother Dyson, whom I had not seen in years.

Each year, we would go to New Mexico to visit my little brothers and their parents, who were such good people, and they would come here as well.

In August 2019, I went to my first Diamondbacks game with Johnny and the kids, and it was so much fun. I was feeling okay; I was still sad but better. Then, the Parkers' oldest daughter, TT, had her twins in August and had become super close.

At the end of September, I found out I was pregnant.

I was so scared. I was told for years that I could not have kids partially because my real mother did all those drugs while being pregnant with me and the trauma I sustained, but at the end of it all, I was feeling so happy.

I wanted to have a family of my own since every family I'd ever had was broken.

I went with my friend Yvette to get an ultrasound.

I got to see the little bean, and so many emotions came through. I told a cousin first, and then my best friend, but who I wanted to tell the most was no longer in my life, so it stung a bit.

I waited to tell Johnny. I wanted it to be a surprise. I got the ultrasound, a pair of booties, and the test, then wrote on it: *boyfriend 2015, husband 2018, daddy 2020.* The emotion on his face with the teary eyes was the same look he gave at our wedding. He was so happy.

His family and friends said he never smiled like that except when his kids were born, marrying me, and then finding out we were expanding the family.

I also found out my girlfriend Dior, whom I worked with at Planet Smoothie, was pregnant.

A month later, I found out Keith and his girlfriend Rachel were expecting also, so she and I became close.

Throughout the rest of 2019, I finally landed a job as a Medical Assistant at a private clinic. It was a good learning experience.

Also, Rachel and I hung out quite a bit.

It was the end of 2019 when I ran into my dad while I was pregnant and driving. I tried to hide, but Javier stuck his head from the backseat and said, "Isn't that your dad?" I drove away but later got a call from him, and he asked how I was doing. I immediately freaked out because I was not sure what to expect. It had been over a year since I'd talked to him.

I just said, "Good," and he asked about my life.

A part of me was like, "Why should you know?

So I told him, "I'm happy and working."

He asked where I was working, and I told him.

After that, I met him for lunch but decided not to tell him I was pregnant.

♥ ♥ ♥ ♥ ♥

Christmas 2019 was a little different for me that year because I spent it pregnant with Aurora and her family since Johnny was out of town for work, but we did a lot of celebrating after he got back.

My doctor gave me a letter with the gender of my baby, which I gave to my sister-in-law. She planned a 'gender reveal' party to be held in January.

That is when I discovered we were having a boy, so Johnny and I were through the roof.

Afterward, I found out my parents were divorcing.

Shawn called me in the middle of January, saying, "Dad asked Mom for a divorce and left."

Being six months pregnant and working, I didn't think I'd ever see my parents again or talk to them, but I became sad for my mom. My older brother asked me to check on our mom because he did not have a car and was worried for her.

Mind you, I hadn't spoken or seen my mom for a few years, and the last thing she said to me was that I was basically nothing and that Johnny should die.

I was hesitant to see her, but I asked my friend, who worked with Dior and was also pregnant, to go with me.

I knew how irrational my mom could be, but since it had been a while and my dad was leaving her, I did not know where her mindset was. She lived on some property, so my brain was thinking the worst.

When we got there, she was not expecting me at all.

She let me and Dior in and looked depressed.

Instead of thanking me for checking on her, she asked me to leave, not wanting my sister to see me.

I took that to mean it was a waste of time coming to check on her, but I did that already knowing how she was towards me. Despite that, I truly cared for her.

I went home sad and cried. It had been an emotional pregnancy for me, and seeing my mom made it harder.

A couple of weeks later, I got into contact with my biological dad. I'd been told he was dying and needed to find out. We maintained a distant relationship as he lived in New York. After all that had already happened, I found out he was on the sex offenders list there.

He was getting taken care of by my Aunt T. because he had been recently diagnosed with Parkinson's and a few other medical issues.

He owned up to everything and even apologized, which helped me move on.

After that, we stayed in contact for quite some time, until he started reverting to his old ways.

♥ ♥ ♥ ♥ ♥

In March 2020, we had what no one knew was about to come to the world: a Pandemic. People were getting sick, and there was really no reason yet for what it was. I became worried about my mom, grandma, and sister and decided to reach out to them. They were doing well.

My dad reached out to me wanting to see how I was doing and even came to my job once to bring me lunch.

He was happy that I was happy but was shocked that I was pregnant.

My mom started coming around with my grandma and sister and introduced me to her boyfriend, Jack.

At the end of April, I was sent home due to being high risk with the pandemic starting.

I ended up not having a job and staying home.

Covid caused schools to shut down and go remote.

My husband's dear uncle was hospitalized due to Covid and was fighting for his life.

My oldest, Javier, started remote learning in April, which changed things. Because of Covid, I did not get to have a baby shower. We were still going to have a little one, but no one wanted to come.

I totally understood, but at the same time, it made me sad. Instead, people did a little drive-by and sent some baby shower gifts to my house.

♥ ♥ ♥ ♥ ♥

The middle of May came, and I kept having false labor, which was painful. Before my baby was born, they kept changing the rules on whether people would be allowed in the delivery room. It changed weekly.

I was scared to do it alone but knew I might have to.

Finally, a few days before I went in, one person was allowed but could not leave. My girlfriend Dior had her baby girl in the middle of May, and she was adorable.

On May 27, 2020, baby Braxton was born vaginally, weighing 7.6 lbs. It was such a blissful moment.

I was in labor for ten hours and pushed for nearly forty-five minutes. The delivery itself wasn't too bad, but the afterbirth is what changed the situation.

I was rushed to the Emergency Room because I was losing a lot of blood. They thought I had torn my cervix.

As I was taken away, I was in and out of it as they were pumping me with medicine. I heard my husband freak out a bit as this was a first for him since the other two he'd witnessed were C-sections.

I was put in a room with my arms strapped out like I was on a cross, lights everywhere, legs open, and the doctor was holding towels of soaked blood.

I ended up passing out and then waking up.

Every time they tried to give me medicine, I threw that up. They finally realized that my uterus was not contracting like it was supposed to and got the rest of the placenta out, which hurt more than the actual birth.

I was then taken back to the hospital room, where I was able to see my baby boy and husband. I held him in my arms, and for that moment, any pain I was feeling or anything that was bothering me just vanished.

He was beautiful.

It is said that some things or people are your saving grace, and I had Johnny and my kids.

Minutes became hours, hours became days, days became months, and months turned into years. Watching my little one every day was such a big blessing.

The first couple of days after my baby boy's arrival, at this point, I was a little hesitant about people coming around him, but I knew time could be gone in the blink of an eye. His grandma, Auntie, Gigi, big brother, and big sister were the first to hold him, and they loved it.

Followed by his Tata, Nana Sylvia, Tio Randy, and his other grandparents, the Farkers. Of course, they had to sanitize their hands beforehand.

I loved seeing everyone interact with him.

His Nana got to hold him as well.

He even got to see my dad, and the interaction was super cute. During all this happy time, our Tio Danny was in the hospital suffering from Covid and later passed away from complications. He was such a great guy and would have loved to meet my little man.

We enjoyed the summer as a new family of five but could not do too much since we were on lockdown from the pandemic.

♥ ♥ ♥ ♥ ♥

As the new school year started, we enrolled Javier in a new school at the start of third grade. Adrianna started her senior year. Both kids had to do online school as schools closed in March due to Covid, so it was a learning experience for many.

The twins had their first birthday in August and were "Thing one and two" themes. It was cute.

My girlfriend TT met Braxton for the first time and loved how big he was and how he stayed in her arms.

In October, we went from a family of 5 to 7 because my daughter's boyfriend asked to move in with us due to things going on in his life. We took in my oldest nephew, Derek, for personal reasons.

My daughter and her boyfriend shared her room after asking permission.

Derek and Javier shared Javier's room, and the little man was in his bassinet in Mom and Dad's room.

With two boys doing online school, our daughter online and working at Taco Bell, her boyfriend working at Taco Bell and going to the University of Arizona, and a baby while my husband was at work, it was a lot.

The boys would fight nonstop, Adrianna and Peter would go in and out of the house between work and school, Johnny would work 2 to 3 jobs to support the family, and there would never be a dull moment here.

We celebrated Halloween together.

My little man and I were koala bears, Javier and Derek were dinosaurs from Jurassic World, and Johnny was dad (lol). He is not big on Halloween.

The boys adjusted to online school, and I adjusted to life as a new mom in a pandemic.

The older ones were experiencing their life, and Johnny was busting his butt.

With Covid going the way it was, the world was changing more and more right before our eyes.

Stores were closing down; things were getting bought in bulk, leaving nothing for others.

Things like toilet paper, formula, and canned foods were cleaned off the shelves. There were a lot of moms who could not get formula for their babies because people were being selfish and buying so many because they did not know when society would open back up again.

We were scared about all of the things going on in the world. All we could do was to pray and leave it to the man upstairs.

November was the election too. So many people thought it was rigged because it was Trump vs Biden, and Biden ended up winning.

Thanksgiving 2020 was different.

I was already accustomed to big family events from Johnny's. We held it at our house, but very few people were present because of the stipulations regarding gatherings during this time.

Braxton had an outfit that said "First Thanksgiving" with a little turkey on his butt. He was doing what we called a gorilla crawl on one leg (lol).

His first word was dada.

We had my mom, grandma, sister, Jack, brother-in-law, and a few family members, and it was nice.

It did feel a little off having my mom there because everything that had been said and done in the past was still in the back of my mind; plus, I had not seen her for almost 3 years, but I felt it was a sign that they were back in my life and it's what I wanted.

My older brother celebrated Thanksgiving with his family as they did not live close and did not have a car.

With Johnny and my anniversary coming up along with Christmas, we were not sure we could celebrate our second anniversary with the pandemic going on.

We could not do our first one either since Johny was out of town for work, so we did a movie at home, made a meal together, and opened a gift from one another.

Christmas 2020 was good.

Johnny was on call about his job with a battery company, and Braxton was seven months old.

We spent Christmas Eve with all the kids, and they went to other family member's house. I went to spend it with my mom at her house. I had been there a few times before, and it was sad, mixed with happiness, because my parents were still together the last time I was there, but the words I was told and the goodbye I got will never leave my thoughts.

The kids got some cool stuff for Christmas, and we adults got some items we loved. To end 2020, we stayed home, drank hot chocolate, had some cake, and loved one another. We were waiting to see what 2021 would bring with the world still on lockdown.

With the new year starting after such a crazy election and the world still going through a Pandemic, it was something we would have to get used to in the next couple of years. There were a lot of changes, we had to wear masks everywhere we went, some people even wore gloves and masks inside their car alone, and we had to stay six feet apart.

For doctors' visits, it was over video or drive-up.

A lot of places were still closed, or hours changed. Schools were still online, and people were still buying things so much that they would be gone.

The first couple of months were all right as I was home with my little one. Derek and Javier were finishing school online, but schools started opening in March. It was the first time the boys took a bus to school, as Derek was not in school, and Javier would get driven. They were in third grade and adapted well.

Adrianna decided to finish her senior year online and graduated.

Braxton turned one in May and had a little party with a dinosaur theme. He was walking more and more and could say, *mama, dada, and hi.*

At Adrianna's graduation, only four people could go because of Covid.

Even Braxton counted, so her boyfriend, Peter, got a ticket from someone else so he could go.

As the summer approached, I was really enjoying 'the mom life' very much. It felt strange not to be working because I had always worked from the age of eighteen until having the baby, but I had to be home during this time. My mom was coming around more with my grandma, sister, and my mom's boyfriend.

She apologized to Johnny about the things she had done and said but never really apologized to me, but I was not expecting that as I was still unsure how our relationship would be. I also had a glimpse of hope in people because I would see the good in them, so I looked past the stuff that had happened.

My dad was talking to me more and more.

He met Braxton several times but still wanted nothing to do with Johnny. I was maintaining a relationship with my biological father as he was doing better and trying to acknowledge the stuff that was done.

I still did not want any communication with my biological mom because not only was she associating with my uncle, but she also played the victim a lot and would never own up to anything.

Javier's birthday was in July.

While there, I learned I would be a Tia again for my sister-in-law, Domonique.

My family and I went to New Mexico as that was our family vacation every year, or my brothers would come down here with their parents.

Summers were very eventful.

In August 2021, Johnny was offered a job with the Tucson Water Department, which he had been praying to get for months. We were both very excited because our family really needed the extra money.

With Braxton getting bigger, Derek and Javier in fourth grade, and Adriana and Peter working and going to college, one relationship that grew stronger was my father-in-law and Johnny's. I grew close to him as well. He has been and still is a good father figure to me.

Johnny said he had not been close to his dad in years, and it gave him a different outlook on everything.

Braxton got to meet his Tia Valerie and enjoyed her.

September was a big month as my daughter and her boyfriend got engaged, and my brother-in-law and his girlfriend got engaged as well.

We were excited for both couples.

By this point, Braxton was playing with his brother, cousin, sister, and soon-to-be brother-in-law.

He loves them all.

As the months went on, we would celebrate each holiday as much as possible during the pandemic.

On Halloween 2021, Braxton was Mickey Mouse, and I was Momma Mouse. The boys were dressed as creepy masked characters. Johnny was dad again (lol).

Thanksgiving was different as we had it at our house with a select few people again and had to do things at the last minute, but it worked out.

We celebrated Christmas Eve with each other and the kids as they went to their mothers' Christmas Day.

I would then go to my brother Shawn's place for a little Christmas with my niece and nephews, and my dad would come down, too.

I discovered my sister-in-law Melody was pregnant again this Christmas and due in June. I also met my dad's girlfriend and got to know her.

Once the holidays were over, more drama ensued in my life. It was something my family and I did not need or want. As 2022 started, my real dad did some things I disagreed with, so I stopped talking to him.

Also, dealing with the loss of a great Tia was traumatic for a lot of people. With this going on, my mom was upset because I was talking to my dad. She was also upset because I was letting him hold my son, which in her opinion, he did not have a right as he was not my blood father. It was a little crazy, but nothing compared to what was yet to come.

In March, my long-time sister Lynette in Louisiana told me she was moving back here with her daughter Addison and divorcing her husband. I was super excited to have her back despite her circumstances.

She moved in with her mother in Three Points.

Braxton's second birthday came. This time, it had a 'Toy Story' theme and was super cute.

Everyone from his first birthday came as well.

Lynette and I got matching tattoos, with the word 'strength' and a heart at the end.

June came, and I became an aunt to Levi.

In July, my stepdaughter and her fiancé married via court online here at the house. School seemed to fly by for Javier. He was in fifth grade and liked his teacher. Lynette met a guy named Kevin and started dating.

My husband and I started hanging out with Yazmin and Adam Montez along the way. They are long-time friends of my husband from his previous job at a tire shop, but I did not become close until last year.

They are super amazing and my favorite couple.

♥ ♥ ♥ ♥ ♥

Other people who have impacted my life are friends who became family, the Bernardo family, the Meyer family, and coworkers of my husbands.

I have never felt so good about having people in my life this long. I would also like to point out that TT is my girl. We hit it off immediately, from not knowing each other only from her parents to having kids a year apart. She has made such a big impact on my life.

It was a decent year until I got a call from my dad.

He wanted to squash the situation with Johnny and put it behind him. I was not sure how I felt about it.

The only thing that was going through my mind was that we were going to my dad's house for a store party and for him and Johnny to talk, and I thought one of them was going to kill the other. I was nervous because of how their relationship was from the anger, hurt, and ugliness that happened.

We got to my dad's, but I was thinking the worst the entire time only because I was scared and knew that just anything could happen. Did I really think the act would happen? No, but you never know what someone can do.

They ended up talking and drinking all night while me and my two boys got food poisoning, so we stayed in bed. By the end of it, I felt relieved because they were able to move past everything and shake hands, which is all I ever wanted. To have my dad support me and be in my life was a good way to end the year.

As the years have passed and everything that I have been through, both bad and good, I sit in silence at times and start feeling depressed. I have never let it get so bad because I saw what it did to the women in my family and did anything I could to prevent it.

Even though people were coming into my life, I was filled with so many emotions because I was still hurt, scared, and feeling vulnerable. I kept myself distracted from the depression with my kids and friends.

Everything seemed to be all over the place, but no life is straight, let alone perfect.

♥ ♥ ♥ ♥ ♥

The following year, we faced a couple of obstacles, but nothing I or my family couldn't handle.

We were living the regular routine life in the Abbot household. Johnny was working nonstop, and Javier was doing school and sports.

Braxton and I stayed home.

He grew increasingly each day.

February 2023 was a heartbreaking month due to losing a friend/sibling. He was only twenty-four and lived life every day, never late to anything, and was an all-around happy guy. With his passing, his parents were beyond heartbroken. I offered to help put the slideshow together and was there daily to support them.

They are the Parkers, as I mentioned in my earlier years. Seeing them go through this and how their oldest TT and I did what we could to ease the burden was sad and made me feel more connected than ever.

I say that because with my blood family and adopted family, I never really experienced such a solid foundation of connection until then. We had his funeral in March, and every month after that, we had them come over for dinner to keep them busy. We would have games, food and more.

As the months went by, Braxton turned three in May, having an Elmo theme, but my mom, sister, and grandma did not come to that party. Lynette and I had become so close that we often hung out.

That summer, we took a trip to New Mexico.

The boys went to Legoland and the aquarium in Phoenix. We also watched a Diamondbacks baseball game with our cousins, Judy and Robert, and their two kids, Veronica and Axel.

Javier had a soccer-themed party, which my dad and his girlfriend attended with other friends/family.

The school year was to begin, and Javier would be starting sixth grade, which he was nervous about since it was a new district, but he adapted very well.

He even received 'Student of the Month' within the second month of school.

Around this time, I felt my relationship with my mom, grandma, and sister was changing because they did not like the idea of me having my dad in my life, especially his girlfriend. I did not talk to them or see them for months. The last party they visited was Javier's tenth event and Braxton's second.

It was not that they had to come, but the reason for them not showing up was what hurt and was hard to explain, especially to my oldest.

I understand not wanting to see an ex or someone you do not like in the same vicinity.

I get like that with Johnny's baby mama.

Then, I became an aunt again to Ryder, the son of my sister-in-law Melody and brother Shawn, and again to Jesus from my brother-in-law Randy and his wife in November.

Braxton started PreK, and I was so nervous for him as he was speech delayed and was not sure how he would do, let alone be treated, but I knew I was getting him the help he needed at an early age, which was far more help than I ever got.

Every other weekend, or at least once a month, we would hang out with the Bernardo, Meyers, Montez, or Arriaga families. Johnny's work crew has become like another family: Keith, Rachel, Lynette, Kevin, my cousin, and the Parkers. Every one of them has taught me that you do not have to know people long to have a relationship or bond.

His work team is the connection: Kris, Michelle, Damon, Destiny, Henry, Chad, Rob, Sonia, Nic, Lou, AJ, Melaine, and Alonso. They became super close, and I would have done anything for them as they would for myself and my family. We would have a few drinks, dance, and events, and it would be fun each time.

That saying people come into your life when you least expect it and make a great impact is the best thing I can use to describe them.

I explained to Javier why my mom and them were not coming around. He understood but did not like it because his mother would do similar things: all of the broken promises, missed games, and lying.

Everyone lies, but to lie after lie, especially to a kid, is not okay. I hated that because my real parents did it to me. I never knew what anything was other than lies.

Even my now parents lie, most often for no reason.

Javier's mother would have excuses as to why she could not see him and so much more, and dealing with that and seeing him go through that and be hurt, I was not going to allow anyone else to break their promises to him or they would not be able to see my kids, family or not. It was hard when our relationship started changing because having my mom constantly again not only messed with me mentally but emotionally.

I did my best to stay composed because of my kids and husband. Johnny knew how I was feeling and did not like me being that way. He said something that I did not like, but in a way, he was right.

"Our life was quieter when they weren't in it."

For the last few months, it was a constant back and forth of "He's not even your real dad, not even blood, he doesn't need you guys in his life" to me talking about how family doesn't mean blood, it's about loyalty and who shows up or whose been there for you.

Sometimes, it upset me because my whole life I was told to choose, or it was done for me. I was not about to do that anymore, so I keep them both in my life because I love them dearly, but I will do what I must for my emotional health and my family.

Christmas was spent with everyone, but it lasted over the span of three days due to our schedules.

Around this time, we discovered my stepdaughter was also expecting her first child. I thought things were on the up from the past couple of years, but little did I know that the next year would be not only heartbreaking but drama-filled. After all, what good is a life without a few broken hearts and drama, right?

At this point, you are probably wondering about Johnny's baby mama and how things turned out for her.

We communicate via text for Javier's sake since he still wants to see his mom and loves her.

She has tried multiple times to get better and does okay, but it does not last long. Johnny and I do not want to keep Javier from his mom, but we would much prefer not to deal with it. Overall, things have subsided with her, and I am doing it because I love Javier and do not want him to grow up to resent his mom for the wrong reasons or any other reason but what he sees.

Finding out Adrianna was pregnant was exciting as I was going to be a Nana and Johnny a Tata, but she and Peter were separated due to their mistakes.

My sister turned 18 in Jan and lost an elderly cousin. She was a sweetheart.

The next month was even harder for me as I found out my biological father passed.

Despite how he was as a parent when I was a child, he apologized and even owned up to things, which made it easier for me to forgive him.

Once I had heard of his passing, I took it super hard, harder than I imagined. I cried every day for a week straight and a couple of times after that.

He was only 59 years old and died of pneumonia, but was alone. When my aunt found him, he was stiff with his eyes open and had been dead for a while.

He suffered from COPD, diabetes, Parkinson's and a life of drugs and it took a toll on his life. I felt horrible as I stopped talking to me over a year ago about something he had done and did not get to say goodbye even though he tried to reach out to me multiple times.

I know I should not feel bad, but I did. Losing him took a piece of me that I did not think I could lose.

My aunt Teresa was the one who found him and let me know immediately.

It took forever to get his death certificate. She sent me some of his ashes, his ID, and some of his favorite knickknacks to split with my brother Shawn.

I talked about his passing on social media, and some people's opinions were not needed.

I know everyone has an opinion, just like everyone has an asshole but sometimes they need to stay hidden. An aunt of mine pretty much told me, he did not deserve my grievance because he was a bad person. I understand the things he did and who he was, but she did not have to be a bitch about it. I knew people like her did not deserve to be in my life.

Regardless of the truth, at a time like that, it should have been left unsaid or sent in a private post.

Following his death, I lost two teachers, two friends, and our Tata. It was a big roller coaster ride.

In March, I got to see Aurora, who I had not seen in months, and we had breakfast for her birthday. It was so good to see her. She has been super sick to where she has had to be incubated a few times. Aurora has been through a lot with me, and I am thankful for her. I also got to see my mom, grandma, sister, and her boyfriend

Jack came by to not just see us, but I had my niece and nephews over, so she got to see her grandkids too.

They brought over gifts and played for a bit.

It was a fun time, but I was still getting asked why I was still talking to my dad.

I was feeling quite frustrated and annoyed at this point, so I just stayed quiet. I love my mom, grandma, and sister very much. I know I will not ever have all my family in one event, but having my parents in my life again has been nice, so I don't want to see that change unless it becomes necessary.

Shortly after this, I discovered I would be an aunt two more times to my sister Lynette and Kevin, my baby brother Wally, and his girlfriend, Yliana.

It seemed there were babies all around me.

Casper has a government job that he really likes and is very happy at the moment.

His and Wally's parents are such great people.

Braxton is talking more and potty trained, knows his ABCs, numbers, and more. He does have a sensory disorder that inhibits his speech, but he is getting better.

I also started talking to my other brother, Steven, whom I have not seen in years, and he is struggling with his health but doing what he can to stay alive with the cystic fibrosis he is battling.

Shawn and I have become super close, like we were as children, even with the fighting.

A wonderful thing happened through all this: I got in contact with an older cousin who is my biological father's cousin, making him my second cousin.

Let us call him Richard. He knew a little bit about my childhood, but by the time he wanted to do something, my real parents had jumped ship again. It was so nice to catch up with him and see him. It did bring back some childhood memories of the abuse that had happened in that short time he was in our life, and that was when it hit me. He was there during the time Tony molested me and made me go down on him, but I could not say anything to anyone as I was told in my head that I would be kidnapped and hurt if I did.

Reliving that memory not only terrified me because I have always been uneasy around people but to still know someone who was supposed to love you took your innocence away in many ways at such an early age. Richard was super supportive when my biological dad passed. He told me childhood stories about my biological dad that were quite interesting. Thinking about some of it gave me a unique perspective on his life.

Within the same month, I found out that my Grammie Chery was not doing well. She had died on the table and came back. Her doctor wasn't sure what happened.

My baby is not a baby anymore as he is turning four and celebrating his birthday baby shark style. It was a good turnout, found out I was going to have a grandson, and Lynette was having a girl. Javier's birthday was Nerf's theme, and it was so fun having water balloons with the adults and even getting involved. I also became close to my cousin Richard and his beautiful, loving wife, Kristine. They are just phenomenal.

I was so happy to have more people in my life who were from my biological dad's side, even though I was warned everyone was bad. My grandson made his entrance on August 1st and found out my little brother was going to have a son. I would like to say I am happy with everyone in my life for several reasons.

They are all in it, bad or good.

One person in my life talks down to me like a child when we are literally a couple of years apart. I am not sure as to why she does this, but it's really changed my perspective on her. I know I may seem timid, but I am not a child first off, and second, I am more level-headed and smarter than she perceives me to be.

Summer came and went, and this year would be one for books because after all these years and for most of my childhood, I was always the person that people stepped on or took advantage of because of how big my heart was and my vulnerability. I analyzed some items that showed me who was there from day one, who only wanted to be in my life when it was convenient for them, and who just used me.

Most people who just got what they wanted ended up being my own family, but by this point, my mom, sister, grandmother, and I have become closer, and I do not want anything to change that.

I learned that the only person who deserves a special place in my life is someone who never made me feel like I was an option in theirs. It is now October of 2024, and here I sit as a 31-year-old mom of three who is married and living a life I never thought possible.

I have developed such beautiful relationships and stronger bonds and even allowed some of the toxicity of people to go.

I still have so much life to live but honestly, I did not think I'd be here today. Through all my hardships, triumphs, traumas, and even good times, it made me the woman I am today. Even though my scars have healed, it does not mean that the pain has, but I am surviving.

I tell myself every day, "You are a survivor."

I am lucky to have survived all the abuse and will continue to survive the recovery.